Master Earth Living

You Can Live Heaven on Earth!

*Allow Jeremy, a Heavenly Light Being,
to show you how.*

**Jeremy Logue, Rhonda Crockett Logue
& Mehrnaz Dehmiri**

Master Earth Living

You Can Live Heaven on Earth!

*Allow Jeremy, a Heavenly Light Being,
to show you how.*

**Jeremy Logue, Rhonda Crockett
Logue & Mehrnaz Dehmiri**

Sprinkling Sunshine

Master Earth Living

Copyright ©2020 by Rhonda Crockett Logue and Mehrnaz Dehmiri
All rights reserved.

Published by Sprinkling Sunshine
www.sprinklingsunshine.com
Oak Hills, California

No part of this publication may be reproduced, stored in a retrieval system, or transmitted in any form or by any means—electronic, mechanical, photocopy, recording, or any other—without the prior permission of the authors.

Cover design by Keshvar Merchant
Cover photo of Jeremy Logue and his Earth girlfriend, Antoniette Ibusag
Editing by Zora Alexandra Knauf

ISBN: 978-1-7339729-0-1

Printed in the United States of America

Acknowledgements

Much love and gratitude to my family and friends, who are always loving and supportive in all that I do. Even though we live in different dimensions, we are always as one and still co-creating together. My mom is out-of-this-world amazing, and I'm so grateful to her for accepting the challenge of creating a second book together and assisting me in sharing my divine wisdom and guidance with you.

I love my Earth dad and siblings—Michael, Nicholas, Rachel, and Megan—for all eternity. I co-create with them every single day, even though they are not always aware of it. We will spend many more exciting lifetimes together.

I am super excited and grateful to have the opportunity to co-create with my friend, Mehrnaz Dehmiri, who added so much wonderful, positive energy and inspiration to our beautiful book. We joyfully co-create together on many projects.

And lastly, I express my sincere gratitude to all our readers for opening your hearts and minds and allowing me to share my love and wisdom with you!

I love you,

Jeremy

Jeremy, a light being in Heaven, channels his divine wisdom and guidance to his Earth mother to present in this book. His Heavenly perspective may not be completely understood by some, and that's OK. Jeremy's wish, though, is for readers to hold an open heart and an open mind, allowing this divine information to be absorbed to uproot the remembrance of one's true essence of divine love.

Reviews

"Jeremy and Rhonda have taken us on a second incredible journey, guiding us on our own paths to find the meaning of our lives and our true spirits. This simple, easy to read and understand guide should be read by all! It's a must read for all awakening now and searching for their true purposes in this lifetime. I recommend both Master Earth Living *and* Jeremy Shares His Love From Above.*"*
— **Tim Mosier**

"I am so grateful for you, Jeremy, and your commitment to help us from the other side. You are such an inspiration. I love the tools in this amazing book that you have shared with us to help us on our journeys of soul transcendence. You have answered so many questions I've had, and now I have peace beyond all understanding. I highly recommend this book to anyone in search of who they really are and why they came to Earth."
— **Marti Browne, Certified Life Coach, Reiki Master/Teacher**

"I am truly honored to have the opportunity to review this incredible book. Jeremy would be the same age as my third son, Daniel, another gift, right now. We are all put here for a reason and have a divine purpose. Some of us fear and resist our own growth, to do the uncomfortable, to take action. This beautiful book enlightens us as to why we are here and to live with purpose and intent, to make a difference, even if it's just to one person or one mission. We all face ups and downs; let's be mindful and raise our vibrations as the book teaches us. You have control—you do. It's your choice to live 'in the misery' or to live your happiest life, and you deserve to live your happiest life. This book teaches us so many things and gives you step-by-step instructions to stay on course, follow your gut, and trust your instincts. This book will show you the way.

"Love to you, Mehrnaz, for sharing and to Rhonda and family, I am truly blessed."

— Randi Goodman, www.randigoodman.com

Master Earth Living

"With this enthusiastic, step-by-step guide on how to optimize one's human experience, living Heaven on Earth becomes a very real possibility. No matter where you are on your spiritual journey, this uplifting story, along with easy-to-follow manifestation techniques, will have you believing in the power of your mind, heart, gut, and breath. An inspiring read that'll leave your soul knowing, 'I can and I will.'"
— **Nadia Jam, MA student in Integral Counseling Psychology CIIS**

"Master Earth Living is truly a beautiful guide for living this earthly life with a heavenly perspective. I felt Jeremy's kind and wise essence as I read each page. As I process a painful event in my life, I will return to this book again and again to remind me how to raise my vibration and be open to spiritual guidance. Jeremy instructs us that it is our mission on this planet to rise above low-vibration feelings in order to be happy and inspire others to do the same. No matter what happens in life, we can return to our natural state of joy!"
— **Jill Hemingway**

Contents

Acknowledgements vii

Reviews xi

Contents xv

Foreword xix

Chapter 1: Do You Know You? 1

Chapter 2: Life's Ups and Downs 5

Chapter 3: Why Don't Heavenly Beings Have Earth Baggage? 9

Chapter 4: Free Yourself Easily by Releasing Low-Vibration Energies 11

Chapter 5: A New Life 13

Chapter 6: Let It Be! 17

Chapter 7: Take Care of You! 21

Chapter 8: The Infinity Chapter 25

Chapter 9: Let Your Light Shine 27

Chapter 10: Write Your Own Book 29

Chapter 11: Follow Divine Guidance for an Easier Earth Life 31

Master Earth Living

Chapter 12: Coincidence or Not? 35

Chapter 12: You Are Unique 39

Chapter 13: Getting into the Flow 41

Chapter 14: You Are the Way! 45

Chapter 15: Light Up the World 49

Chapter 16: Your Mission in Life 51

Chapter 17: It Is Your Birthright to Live Joyously and Free 53

Chapter 18: The Art of Playing 55

Chapter 19: Just Be You! 57

Chapter 20: Everything's the Way It Is Supposed to Be! 59

Chapter 21: Is Your Spirit Within? 63

Chapter 22: Hear Me and Hear Me Big! 67

Chapter 23: It Is Time! 69

What to Do When Your Mind Runs the Show 71

Afterword by Jeremy Logue 73

Afterword by Rhonda Crockett Logue 75

Afterword by Mehrnaz Dehmiri 77

Other Books by Jeremy Logue 79

Master Earth Living

You Can Live Heaven on Earth!

Foreword

Hi, I'm Jeremy! I passed from this lifetime on June 20, 2016 in a car accident. I passed quickly and I was greeted by my grandmother who passed a few months before I did. My family and friends on Earth were very sad, but a few years prior, my mom learned how to listen to divine spirits, and this brought some comfort and peace.

Right away, I began communicating to my mom through her thoughts, her vision, her knowing, and any way that I could to get her attention. The day of my passing, I kept making an old cell phone of mine go off. My mom thought the music it played was beautiful. She'd never heard it before. No one could understand how the phone continued to ring each time when it was turned off.

I communicated through my mom to give messages to my family and friends—to let them know that I was OK. My mom wrote down what she heard from me. She knew it was information from me because these messages weren't things she would say. My mom hears me in her head but doesn't usually experience it like someone's voice. It's hard to explain until you experience it yourself. Sometimes she just has a knowing about something, and she knows it came from me.

Master Earth Living

My mom, my Earth girlfriend, and I created our first book, *Jeremy Shares His Love From Above,* to help folks transition through the loss of a loved one to finding peace and living a joyous life.

I have so much more to share with you to assist you with living a Heavenly Life while on Earth. I loved my 18 and a half years of Earth life and I believe I lived it well. Now I am on a divine mission to enlighten wonderful beings like yourself to live the amazing life you chose to live before you came to Earth.

So, sit back, relax, drink a cup of coffee, and enjoy as I guide you to living your best Earth life yet!

Chapter 1
Do You Know You?

Do you know yourself? Know who and what you are? Know why you are here and what you are here for? Do you know you?

When you arrived in body on this planet, you knew exactly who and what you were. Did you forget? Many do. Knowing who you are usually becomes lost early on when you experience Earth life, which can consist of trauma and unpleasant circumstances. We tend to forget who we really are.

So, who are you? Well, you are a divine being who chose to have a life experience on this planet we call Earth. We all chose this, but why? We chose this because we wanted to evolve. Our beings are always in motion, moving forward. Sometimes we are moving very slowly, but we are always moving to our desired purpose. Your soul, spirit, or inner being (whichever term you would like to use) knows the specifics of your desired divine purpose. However, whatever your specific purpose may be, every soul's mission is always to evolve in certain areas. To grow is to live.

Fear is resistance to growth. Resistance can be painful because our spirits came to Earth to live and experience the goodness of life. However, on Earth

Master Earth Living

we have the mind, or the ego, attached to our Earth bodies, and our minds fight vigorously at times to remain stagnant. You may have noticed a small voice inside that told you, "You're not good enough"; "You can't do it"; or "It will never happen for you." This is the Earth mind or ego talking, instilling fear and untruths, stagnation, and resistance to growth.

The mind was initially supposed to observe, but somewhere along most of our Earth journeys, we allowed fear to take over. We chose to believe the untruths told to us by others, and then we chose to not live completely from our hearts. Ultimately, we began resisting our own divine guidance. We allowed our controlling minds to take over, which resulted in a fear-based existence, deterring us from living as the loving beings that we are.

We cannot blame our minds; they have just been protecting us the best they know how. We can, however, be enlightened to this illusion and rise above to live from our hearts once again, living our life purposes that we came here to live.

So, who are you? You are a divine light being, connected to your infinite source, which many call God, Source, Buddha, etc. The strength of your connection to your higher source is up to you. You are a divine light being embodied in an Earth form, having an experience on Earth. The mind and the ego are attached to the body, so this just comes with the package deal. However, you can master the

Master Earth Living

Earth mind and live Heaven on Earth. We will learn how in upcoming chapters.

Why are you here? You are here to experience, to learn, to grow, to evolve, to be happy, and to master Earth life as a divine light being living in an Earth body.

Chapter 2
Life's Ups and Downs

Your life will have its ups and downs, but you get to choose if you want to be up or down throughout the process. Yes, that's right. You get to choose.

My parents are learning to take everything in stride. Everything that occurs is positive for our growth, even what might not seem so positive. Maintaining a positive attitude is not always easy to do, as many times we return to our Earthly state of mind, holding onto every emotion that comes our way from the perceptions we derive from an Earthly experience. But I'm telling you, you will find peace, joy, and bliss living on a Heavenly level while on Earth.

"What is the meaning of living on a Heavenly level?" you ask. It is living with the awareness that you are a loving being of the Universe and you can exert love into every Earth situation you choose to involve yourself in.

Here's an example. My loved ones on Earth chose to play a part in my transitioning from my Earth life. This was in our soul contracts that we had divinely created prior to incarnating on Earth. Many viewed my transitioning as a negative event, but all involved were to learn from this experience, which enriched

Master Earth Living

their lives. My mom gained a greater understanding of life, transitioning, the divine, and so much more. She now assists others to live their true divine selves while on Earth and in doing so she maintains a close connection to where she came from, which is home—or Heaven, which many have named it.

Awareness is essential to living in Heaven on Earth. I suggest hanging around positive people who are living in the light and living joyous lives so that this way of life becomes familiar to you and you can recognize it as something you want for yourself. It's all a choice, but enlightenment and awareness assist you in making the choice that your soul or spirit desires.

Have you ever wondered why some people have depression and illnesses and what my mom calls "Earth Baggage"? When you are near this type of person, do they share hope and positivity, or do they drain your energy with hopelessness and negativity?

Awareness assists in recognizing that a person can change their attitude with the change of their perception of a situation.

Illness is your soul informing you it's time to wake up, smell the coffee or roses, and get on the positive track of life, letting go of the Earth Baggage. Remember what your soul already knows—you are here to live your life on Earth in joy and peace, radiating love in every situation, knowing that all situations are for your own growth and expansion.

Master Earth Living

So, what changes will you make in your life today? When you change your attitude, you change your life. You know that song "All About That Bass" by Meghan Trainor? My dad loves that song, and my mom thinks he's weird. But seriously, it's all about vibration and frequency. You can choose a positive attitude, a high vibration, and to love life, which will attract more positive experiences, or you can choose a negative attitude, a low vibration, and a sad life, which will attract ailments and misfortune.

What do you choose?

Chapter 3
Why Don't Heavenly Beings Have Earth Baggage?

Well, Heavenly beings radiate at a level of higher vibration than Earth Beings. So, raise your vibration. Aside from me, has anyone ever told you that? What is vibration? What am I talking about? Vibration is frequency. Vibration is movement. Vibration is energy. Energy is moving. High vibration is faster movement, and low vibration is slower movement.

What do you feel like when your movement is slow? Does it feel like you're walking in quicksand or stuck in place? Not such a great feeling. When our energy is vibrating slowly, we tend to acquire ailments and depression. Ailments and depression vibrate at a low frequency, and you are actually attracting these things if your vibration is low. Not such a wonderful way to live.

But, on the other hand, there is high-vibration energy, which is faster moving energy. When your energy is high, do you get more things done? Do positive thoughts come your way? Do you feel a sense of accomplishment, and are you eager to do more? Does life appear happy and loving?

Well, when your energy is on high, you are

Master Earth Living

attracting high-vibration energy, which includes love, positive thoughts, positive people, and positive circumstances. Is this a cool way to live or what? You attract the frequency that you emit.

Bottom line is you get to choose which frequency, or channel, that you want to live on. Low frequency (vibration)—CNN. Yuck! or high frequency—the Discovery Channel. Yippee!

Life in Heaven is on the high-frequency channel. Low-frequency emotions of sadness and sorrow do not last long in Heaven because we are close to our Source (God) energy, which is always high and always loving. Our lower vibrations just fall away. Heavenly beings continuously emit loving energy to their Earth families in the form of assistance and guidance.

So, since you get to choose which type of frequency you want to vibrate on, what do you choose for today? Remember, your days are numbered on Earth, so choose wisely. Those who choose to live in Heaven on Earth have made a decision to see good in all things, just as their Source always does. Always! Trust me on that!

Take this a step further and allow all low-vibration energy to leave. You'll learn how to do this in the next chapter.

Chapter 4
Free Yourself Easily by Releasing Low-Vibration Energies

First, you must recognize where your vibration level is at by how you are feeling. Are you feeling sad, depressed, tired, and bored? Then your energy is vibrating at a low level. So, what can you do?

Well, you have to decide if you want to raise your vibration or remain where you are at. It's your choice. Making the choice to raise your vibration is the first step, and it is a crucial one. So good for those who choose the high-vibration way—living with freedom; living Heaven on Earth.

OK, now you want to identify which low-vibration emotion is holding you hostage. Is it sadness? Is it hatred? Is it irritability? Whatever it might be, state what it is. Now detect where in your energy field this emotion feels the heaviest. Is it your head? Your leg? Just ask and listen; feel or sense what area you are directed to.

When we experience a low vibration in our energy field, it begins to permeate a certain area of the body and wreak havoc. If left unattended long enough, this low-vibration energy creates dis-ease. So, let's get rid of it.

Master Earth Living

An example of this might be feeling the emotion of sadness and also feeling soreness in your leg. You might think that the emotion and the ailment are unrelated, but often they are. Once this information is determined, this issue has been brought to the surface, and divine forces, along with your intent to let go of this energy, go to work to release and regain stability and balance.

Simple, right? Well, it really is this simple if you want it to be—it's your choice!

Now, for many, it might be easier to discover a discomfort or ailment within the body and then determine the emotion that goes with it. Either technique is good. Then, with your intention, allow it to leave. Be free!

And that's how you do it. Simple. Practice this daily. Set your intention of what you want. Every time a negative thought comes up, recognize it and count backwards from 17 to 0. Once you get the hang of these techniques, you are on your way to higher-frequency living. Now give it a try.

You are a child of the Universe and you deserve to live in a high-frequency state of love and light, which is living Heaven on Earth! Your divine loved ones in Heaven are always nearby to assist. Just ask for their assistance and release, let go, auf wiedersehen, au revoir, adios, good riddance, and good-bye.

Everything is divinely perfect!

Chapter 5
A New Life

A new life. A new way of living. Living Heaven on Earth. You can do it. Everything is peaceful. Almost at a standstill. Quiet. All you see is beauty. Beauty everywhere—even in what once was considered conflict. Beauty in all people, places, and things. Breathe it in. If this is what you want, I'll tell you how to get it.

In the previous chapter you released heavy energies. On Earth that will be an ongoing process, but you will become very good at it to the point that you will not even notice the unpleasantness of it any longer. When you release, you open yourself up for the goodness, the beauty, the peace that you seek. The more you allow yourself to release, the greater the amount of space to experience the joy that your soul truly desires. This is really cool.

Just imagine walking down the street and witnessing two young men having an argument or disagreement. You smile. They see your smile, and you're vibrating energy of peace and love. Then watch what happens. Even if the young men do not see your smile, they will feel your presence. Your presence of joy radiating out to them with the intent to remind them of who they are. Reminding them

Master Earth Living

they are rays of light as your light is igniting their light. We are all connected. All of our energies affect one another.

If you are near a person who is sad, then smile. They will feel you. Our energy is powerful and connects on a soul level. Many, I mean most people on Earth, need to be reminded who they truly are, which is a being of infinite light and love energy. So, shine your light brightly, assisting others to remember who they are at the core.

When one lives on this level, one is living Heaven on Earth. There is nothing on Earth that can affect them, as they are walking with divine light beings. The more one can live from this true perspective of love, beauty, and joy, well, yes, you guessed it, the more that person will experience what they are radiating out. And what one radiates outward is a complete validation of what they are radiating inward.

It is time to allow all the strife, the struggle, the pain, and the ailments to release. Bid them farewell. We are all children of our divine maker, and we have great missions to accomplish on Earth. You can't accomplish your mission to your satisfaction when you are weighed down with heaviness.

Free yourself, let your light shine, vibrate with intention to a higher level through awareness and grace, and affect others to do the same. We are working as a team here on Earth, helping one

Master Earth Living

another to master these skills and to live amazing Earth lives in joy, peace, and love.

Chapter 6
Let It Be!

Learn the art of allowing. You can't receive if you do not let it be! *What does he mean by that?* you may wonder. If you are trying to control everything instead of just letting it be, then you will not receive what you desire because you are not allowing. Actually, you may receive the opposite of what you desire, including chaos and confusion. When you let go, you allow and then are in the position to receive what you desire.

It's like this: when riding on a bus, do you let the bus driver drive, or do you bother the driver about his driving? You probably don't even pay attention to the driver as you play on your phone or look out the window. You just arrive at your destination safely.

What if you allow your maker to lead the way? What if you allow your higher source to move you in the direction of your desires? Typically, when an uncomfortable or terrifying event occurs, we think, *What can I do to correct this?* instead of just allowing it to be and moving gracefully through it, trusting that our higher source knows how to get us to where we want to be.

If you experience a breakup with a partner and start getting down on yourself, the flow of divine wisdom is not heard. Why? You're not letting it be. You might be asking yourself, *What can I do to fix this?* But, this situation was created just for you; for your overall growth and wellbeing. When you maneuver through the storm with trust and faith, you know that your desire for a wonderful relationship with a partner is in the works and headed your way. It's all in divine timing and for your best interest and evolution.

So, in the midst of a difficult situation, say to yourself, "I will ride this through, learning from all involved, growing in my faith and completely trusting that my higher source is guiding me and leading me through the storm to the other side to my desires."

Easy, right? No, not always. But the more that you trust in your higher source, the easier it becomes. Now I'm not saying to sit back and do nothing while a storm is raging around you; be observant of your surroundings and good to yourself. Know that everything is divinely planned for our benefit. Everything!

Allow, listen, and act on your intuition, which is your divine guidance—that little still voice in you that says, "Move towards happiness." Often we do not act on the divine guidance we receive, and the storm tends to stick around longer. If you are not happy, then you are not divinely where you are supposed to be, and you have chosen a bumpy path

Master Earth Living

with resistance instead of allowing and letting it be.

Follow your heart. Follow your bliss. Then you are truly free. You can never go wrong with this, as you are in complete "let it be" divine flow. Everything you need is in front of you. Follow your happiness and you will see. Let it be!

Chapter 7
Take Care of You!

As you venture through Earth life's ups and downs, highs and lows, it can create wear and tear on the emotional and physical body. Until you master Earth living and riding above the tide (or chaos)—instead of getting stuck in it and then maneuvering your way out—Earth living can take a toll on you. That is why it is so important to take care of yourself!

Nourish yourself with good food, healthy food. Produce like fresh fruits and vegetables is the best, as foods from plants provide a grounding effect with Mother Earth. Your body will feel so much better when you incorporate colorful produce into your diet. I'm sure you have noticed a change in your or others' emotional and physical energy following eating a Big Mac from McDonalds, which may lower one's vibration, as opposed to eating high-vibration fruits and vegetables. Low-vibration foods can feel heavy and stagnant while high-vibration foods can feel energetic and alive.

Clean water is great for flushing out toxins. Earthly bodies experience stress, toxins, and unhealthy products that can create health issues. So, drink lots of water.

Spend time in nature. Reconnect with that part

Master Earth Living

of you that loves the great outdoors. Plant a garden. Smell the roses. Have gratitude for all of God's beautiful creations. It is all here for you, and it is a wonderful way to rejuvenate your mind and body.

Guard yourself with divine light. It is available to you 24-7. Just for you and all who care to utilize it. Envision a beautiful bright light blazing down from above, like the bright sunshine embracing you in a warm comfy blanket on a chilly night. Feel the love that it has for you. Breathe it in. It is pure love. The more you surround yourself with divine light, the more smoothly your Earth life will go because this divine light protects one from toxins produced by others. So, get into the light.

Remove yourself from all toxic people. I know that this isn't always possible, but try your best. By doing so you maintain your balanced energy, focus, and emotional stability. Then, when you do encounter toxic people, their energy will not affect you like it once did.

Always maintain a close connection with divine beings. This is done by allowing them to be a part of your life. As a society, most are taught to resist divine help. But it is a choice. Choose to feel and see your divine connection with us Heavenly beings. We are happy to hold your hand, to lead and to guide. Call on your Heavenly angels anytime. We love you!

Engage in uplifting activities that make you smile. My fun Earth activity was to go to the beach

Master Earth Living

with my beautiful girlfriend, listen to the waves crashing, and sit around the bonfire until late at night. I enjoyed this so much and I didn't want this high-vibration feeling to end. I was totally and completely connected with my higher source and living Heaven on Earth during those moments. When you engage in activities you love, your soul is rejoicing. Make sure you do not skip this step in self-care. Plan a fun activity in your schedule every day, writing it in your daily planner so that it happens. You will be glad that you did.

Beach trip – Jeremy and his girlfriend, Antoniette

You can glide smoothly through Earth life when you practice what I have shared. The lows will then not seem so low, and you will be more focused on living on a Heavenly level on Earth. Your awareness of what is happening is heightened, including why things are the way they are and what you need to do to maintain that Heavenly vibration while living on Earth.

So, take care of you! Call on us! Listen, observe, know, and feel our guidance, and you will be riding on top of the Earth wave that previously felt like

Master Earth Living

chaos. Hopefully, you now know that all is divinely planned for your evolution.

Chapter 8
The Infinity Chapter

You can have anything that you desire. If you can think of it, you can have it. Most people do not believe this, and that is their roadblock to receiving the abundance that is available for them. You came to Earth to live, to live a great life, and to live an enlightened life. Living in poverty, hunger, and limitations—is that a great life? I don't think so.

Let me show you how this all works. Dream an idea. An example might be wanting a million dollars. Ask yourself, *What would I do with a million dollars?* Keep dreaming... *I would buy a boat. I would travel the world. I would help the less fortunate*...if such a concept really exists (lol), as every person is an infinite being with infinite possibilities! Feel into your dream, your desire of what having a million dollars feels like. Do you feel happy and excited? Are you having the time of your life? It's your life. It's your dream. Enjoy this feeling and come back to this feeling several times each day because your dream is beginning to take form.

Now if thoughts like *this isn't possible* or *I don't deserve this* arise, this means you are getting in your own way (the ego Earth mind) of your dream coming to life. So, get out of your way. You deserve

Master Earth Living

what you want. You are on Earth to live a wonderful life.

The more that you envision and feel your dream, the more quickly it can evolve into reality. Now, while you are in your dream, listen to your divine guidance. You will hear messages, like instructions that may inform you that an acquaintance of yours is looking for a person who can offer exactly your talent. Your talents are your gifts, so be open to their call. Maybe you receive a message that a certain business interest is going to be a great investment and that you should continue to pursue it. Maybe a long-lost relative has passed and left their multi-dollar home to you, and their attorneys have been unable to reach you. Make contact for details, listen to what your divine guidance has to say, and follow their instructions. The divine is always working on your behalf to bring about your desires.

It's funny how the divine communicates with you. You may just have a clear understanding, or you may hear a message in a song or from another person. Just be open to receive. This is real, guys. This is the truth. I would not steer you wrong.

Have you ever had a gut feeling about something? Yep, it was divine guidance. So, follow it and move on, creating your wildest desires (Dream big!) and make sure you share how to do this with all who you know. It's a win-win situation.

Chapter 9
Let Your Light Shine

This little light of mine, I'm going to let it shine. Let it shine, let it shine, let it shine! We are all shining stars in our own Universe; stars of our own show. The galaxy is filled with shining lights. Some shining bright and some not so bright. It's a choice as to how bright to shine. Here are those choices again. Lol. Do you choose to shine bright, or do you choose to dim your light?

You might be wondering, *What exactly is my light*? Well, it is your connection to your maker, your higher source, source energy, God, whatever term you choose to use. It's all the same. This divine energy is you, and you get to choose how much of it you want to allow in and shine. Choosing to shine brightly consists of walking in bliss, allowing the divine to lead, sharing your gifts, and knowing all is well and right in the world and in the Universe. Living peacefully. Choosing not to shine brightly may consist of struggle. Struggle is the best term for it. Not following your divine guidance, off your path, nothing working out, frustrated and unhappy. Not living peacefully.

Master Earth Living

You are a divine being of the Universe, glowing on the inside, ready to express yourself and expanding. Your light actually is quite difficult to hold back. Some of you have mastered blocking your light, though. But you are ready, and the time is now to set your light free and be all that you came to Earth to be. A beacon of light for others to see, radiating your love passed down from above. Let go of all fears. Just let that crap go. You are here to live and to grow with your light expanding far out beyond the horizons. Now you know.

Chapter 10
Write Your Own Book

If you had the pleasure of reading my first book, *Jeremy Shares His Love From Above*, you know that I had two Chapter 10s because when you write your own book, or your mom listens and writes it for you, you can do anything you want.

The number 10 breaks down to 1+0=1, and my fist book, *Jeremy Shares His Love From Above*, was the one and only book you needed to live a joyous life on Earth...until this one! This book has two Chapter 12s, and I bet you can't wait to get to Chapter 12s to find out why.

But, anyhow, I want you to write your own book, your book of your journey, your life, the lessons you've learned, and where you were and where you are now. It's a beautiful journey about you. Everyone's journey is unique and special. There are no two journeys that are the same. There can't be. Many can learn from your journey and apply what is useful to their own, but their journeys will still be different than yours.

Your journey is a blessing, a magnitude of miracles. Most miss the many miracles, but they are still there to receive. Your life is a miracle. Every day is a blessing. It is a new day to explore, live, expand,

Master Earth Living

and to love. A day to be guided on your path of divine love, which is you.

The gift of life is to be treasured, valued, and loved. No matter what you had previously planned for your life in your "soul contract (life plan)," value and treasure all that comes to you, even if it is the Earth death of a loved one. What most Earth people don't understand so well is that even though you cannot see a loved one who has passed or transitioned, they are still present to feel and hear if you allow it.

In all passings, there is great meaning and growth. My mom blossomed into sharing her amazing gifts with the world. This was our plan, our soul contract. And, of course, I'm helping to guide and assist each step of the way, as loved ones in Heaven do.

Your life is a miracle, so don't miss the blessings that can fulfill your day. Every day is a blessing! Everything is a blessing! You are the miracle that you seek!

Chapter 11
Follow Divine Guidance for an Easier Earth Life

You have free will to do what you like, but your soul wishes for you to follow the light, the divine light, your divine guidance. Earth life is so much easier when you do. Your divine guidance consists of angels, ancestors, deceased friends, guides, God, Buddha—just to name a few.

So, how best to connect?

Well, that is different for each person, but the key element is to know that you can. You actually already are connected, and one way that divine guidance can come to you is through the gut. Isn't that weird? The solar plexus chakra, located in the stomach area, is a portal to divine guidance. So, listen to your gut! You've heard that before, right? Your gut will steer you in the right direction every time.

If you feel sick in the gut, then you are off from your divine path. You are not listening to divine information! So, to get back on your divine path, discover what brings you pleasure and do it. It could be listening to music, hiking, gardening, or dancing. Whatever brings you pleasure will put you back on your divine path. Your gut, your divine connection, is

Master Earth Living

truthful and it will never steer you wrong.

This may sound weird, but the umbilical cord was your divine connection to us Heavenly beings and still is. It's almost like when the umbilical cord is cut at birth, the line becomes partially closed to the divine so that you can make your way on Earth. But no worries! The divine connection remains even though the physical umbilical cord was cut because the energetic umbilical cord is still intact. This divine connection is now one of trust rather than a physical connection.

You don't need to understand this concept, as it is confusing to the Earth mind. My mom is trying to understand as she writes what I share and looks a bit baffled. All you need to know is that you are connected to divine guidance all the time, everywhere, and even when you feel that you are not. Faith, baby! Have faith! Trust in what you cannot see with your eyes.

So, listening to your gut is the easiest way to connect to us, your divine guidance. Then it is whatever you are open to and allow. Do you want to hear us or see us? It's your preference. My mom likes to hear us and she follows her knowing as well. Her knowing is ideas that just seem to randomly pop into her mind. She is enlightened and ready for information that we share. Most others prefer to see and feel divine energy.

It doesn't matter which method you prefer. What

Master Earth Living

matters is that you trust and grow your connection with your divine guidance. We are the light! You are the light! And together we can shine very bright. This is significant because when we shine brightly, others receive our light, which is guidance and support; which is LOVE!

So, practice first listening to your gut and following its divine guidance. Then choose your preference to hear, know, or see, and then delight. Maintain your strong faith in whichever method you choose and go forth, my dear friend. Go and spread your divineness with the world!

Chapter 12
Coincidence or Not?

This is my favorite chapter because—you might remember this fact from my first book, *Jeremy Shares His Love From Above*—the number 12 is my favorite number. Did you know that a soccer ball has 12 pentagons in its truncated icosahedron shape, which is like 12 faces on a soccer ball? Soccer was my

Jeremy plays his favorite sport with his favorite number, 12, on his jersey.

Master Earth Living

favorite sport that I had played since I could walk, and I wore the number 12 on my jersey as often as I could.

So my question is...do you think it's a coincidence that I loved the number 12 and the number 12 was involved in the shape of the soccer ball, a sport that I loved? Nope, it is not a coincidence. It has meaning, and it was meant to be. The number 12 is all powerful, is associated with magic and leadership, and it was me.

Situations that seem like coincidences are not coincidences at all. They are divinely planned by you and your divine helpers to bring meaning, enlightenment, and growth. When you randomly end up somewhere and run into a favorite friend, or maybe a not-so-favorite friend , it is not a coincidence. It was meant to be. You are just assisting in another's journey, and another is assisting in your journey. So, relax and enjoy the ride. Know that everything is for you, by you, to aid in your divine growth. So, glide through. Don't question. Just receive.

My mom was allowing her mind to run wild. You all know how that is. LOL. But a CD magically turned on by itself. It was a healing CD with musical tones to awaken and grow. My mom smiled and didn't question much except to say that I had turned it on because the remote was sitting by my senior picture on the mantle. I was in Heaven at the time this occurred. But she relaxed, cleared her mind, felt peaceful, and smiled. Was it a coincidence? Nope. It was divinely planned, and it was me.

Think about how many times occurrences like these happen and we just blow them off as strange, weird, and "just a coincidence." Time to stop this. Know that it was divinely planned for you along with all others involved. Everything is as it is, as it should be, and it is perfect. Love your journey.

Chapter 12
You Are Unique

My favorite number again. Twelve is the number of the ascended masters, just like me. Only kidding. I'm enlightened and working on ascended-master status, just as we all are. That's what we do. We live in body or purely in spirit form, and we grow, expand, and evolve. That's what it's all about...getting to the most peaceful spot on our love journey. We are all undeniably love. Love for ourselves and all of God's creations. Love! Just love!

The rainbow in the sky represents the many colors of us all. We are all light and we are all uniquely ourselves. There is no one else just like you. Even twin flames are still unique. God is the mastermind of all creations, and we are all uniquely beautiful in our own way.

With that being said...your divine gifts are unique as well. No need to compete or feel that another's gifts are greater than your own. You can't compare. You are different. You are unique, and so your gifts that you share are unique as well.

Love being you. There is no one else in the universe who can speak, sing, or talk like you. No one. They can try and come close, but nope, can't do it. It doesn't work that way.

Master Earth Living

We are all enlightened, moving towards ascended-master status like Jesus and Buddha, working towards the same goal. We're just doing it in our own unique way. So cool! Just keep shining and sharing your true divine self, and then you are doing well. We love to support you, just as you support us as well. We are all in this together. Shine bright!

Chapter 13
Getting into the Flow

This has a nice ring to it—getting into the flow. It's like following the tone of a bell. Getting into the flow where all things are possible. Many have named this the Vortex. A place where you have placed all the exciting events, people, and things that you wish to bring forth into your physical world.

My Heavenly buddies and I want you to know how true this is. You have planted many, many wonderful things into your individual vortex. You did most of the planting before you entered the physical realm, or Earth, or any other planet. In fact, you likely filled your vortex many lifetimes ago, and it's all good.

But the million-dollar question is how to get that beautiful relationship, that nice car, or that magnificent vacation out of your vortex and into your physical world.

First and foremost, you must remember that you can. Bring this concept into your awareness so that you consciously know that your vortex is real.

Second, you must breathe, breathe, and breathe. You will most likely have resistance arise, or disbelief, and the quickest way to turn off the negative mind is to breathe. If you're like my mom, who forgets to breathe, to breathe deeply, then set your phone alarm so that it reminds you to breathe deeply for four or more breaths every hour. This helps to clear out those negative, distracting thoughts that remind us what we don't want.

Third, reach for what you desire. It's already in your vortex. Let me prove it to you.

Have you had a constant thought about something you wanted? Maybe a romantic partner or a dream house? That is your soul just throwing you little messages, reminding you can have all that you desire, as it is already in your vortex. If it wasn't in your vortex, you wouldn't be thinking about it. Love the process. So, focus and give attention to a couple of things you desire. For example, if you desire a dream home, then start being observant and openly start looking for it. I guarantee you will find it, or it will find you. Because whatever you are seeking is seeking you. And no worries—you don't have to know how your desire will surface; we will lead you there. Just start moving your intentions and actions to having what you want and let us do our part.

Fourth, let's say you found your dream home. Always be open to something even better, as we see better from our Heavenly view than is possible from your Earth view. Stay open for what comes your way and move, go, and take action on your divine-inspired messages. We throw them to you constantly, and remember from my first book, we send messages in many creative ways—in songs, messages from others, radio announcements, your knowing, and so many more. Just stay open and when you receive our guidance, run with it. We are showing you the way, guiding and supporting you throughout the process.

Fifth and lastly, we must discuss the mind or ego again and those negative thoughts that will rise up. First, know that the negative thoughts of *I don't deserve...*, *I can't do it*, and *It will never happen for me* are not real. All that is real is your loving supportive thoughts, cheering you on and championing you as you evolve. So, just tell those negative thoughts, "Thank you, but take a hike. I am on a divine mission to happiness!" Then allow those negative thoughts to move on and refill with our divine love and support. We love assisting you in obtaining all your desires into your physical realm. Oh, and one last thing, give thanks. We love gratitude and we love you!

Chapter 14
You Are the Way!

Through you, we share and reach more people in need of support and guidance. Your Heavenly loved ones want to assist and to guide their loved ones on Earth. They have many loved ones from many lifetimes they are closely connected to. We all are connected but more closely connected to our loved ones with whom we have shared
many lifetimes.

Through you our light shines. Many times, when a loved one transitions, our path takes a new direction. I know for my mom, she never in her wildest dreams thought she would be channeling me and writing a book. That was not in her awareness until I passed. Then it surfaced. She could hear me and she began writing to communicate better with me. And though her path had changed, the ultimate gift was for her to evolve. And that she has done.

You are the way you are no matter which path you are on. We, your Heavenly loved ones, shine through you, above you, and around you to help you to reach the stars and to help others to reach their stars. We are all in this together, raving and cheering each other on as we all reach new heights in our beingness.

My mom likes the word "beingness," which to her holds the meaning to just be and to allow your divine being to shine. How beautiful is that? It's like a beautiful flower blossoming or the moon shining bright in the night. A coming out. An awakening. It's beautiful when a human being begins to shine. And you definitely know when a person is that way. They smile from ear to ear. They glow. They are self-assured and confident; in the flow and loving every aspect of life.

Have you noticed how pregnant women exhibit a beautiful glow? The small divine being growing inside of them is shining their divine light, and the mother to be is allowing that to be. When resistance occurs or a pregnant woman blocks the light of her divine baby (and this is not usually done consciously), then illness or what you call morning sickness occurs. Isn't it funny how morning sickness usually disappears by about the third or fourth month of pregnancy? Well, by the third month, the mother usually stops resisting and allows the light of her unborn child to mesh with her own. Then she begins to glow. All is divinely planned for the growth of all involved.

So, you are the way, the divine way. We shine through you, assisting and guiding when you allow us to, and together we shine bright, paving the way

Master Earth Living

for others to follow. So cool, right?

With this awareness, choose to allow our light in and then watch as the magic begins.

Chapter 15
Light Up the World

As we all come together in divine clarity, sparkles of light arise. A once sad, depressed man shows a glimmer of hope in his eyes. The devastated woman whose child is now in Heaven finds peace and joy in seeing a reflection of her son or daughter within herself. A child who sits all alone uncovers his wounds to find the love and peace that he seeks.

Your divine light ignites others' divine lights, and others' divine lights do the same. This is known as the ripple effect. Helping just one person has a profound effect on all of humanity. Divine light is heartfelt on many levels. Ailments surface to address and to release in their own timely manners. Depression, poverty, and conflicts all do the same.

Shine your divine love and light on each issue that arises. Then love it, as all issues were divinely planned for you. Thank it for helping you to grow, and then allow the issue to move on so that you are clear to shine your light bright.

When we help ourselves, we are helping so many others. As my mom often shares, "Your light touches the souls of others, releasing their resistance to their own divine light." We in Heaven are cheering you on. You are doing great work with great love, and the

Master Earth Living

world is a better place because of you.

Chapter 16
Your Mission in Life

Your mission in life is to be happy and inspire others to do the same. "But why is my Earth mission to be happy?" you might ask. Well, let me first ask you, how does your mind, body and spirit feel when you are happy? How do others feel in their minds, bodies, and spirits when they are happy? Happy, right? This is a great high-vibration feeling that trumps all those low-vibration feelings of sadness, anger, illness, etc. So, your Earth mission is to be happy and inspire others to be happy because then you have risen above sadness, anger, and even illness, even if only for a short time. When in the state of happiness, all problems that once existed seem smaller, and ideas and solutions tend to flood into the mind.

Have you ever received an idea or felt energized to solve a problem? Well, you were most likely in a high-vibration state of happiness, love, or gratitude when the wonderful idea arrived. This is why our Earth mission is to be happy and inspire others to be happy so that problems, ailments, and negative situations resolve quickly and life is blissful. And inspiring others to be happy has a ripple effect on our planet, as I have already shared, where all things are possible.

Master Earth Living

In my Earth life, I tried to be happy most of the time, and I inspired others to be happy, but it wasn't always easy to maintain this high state of happiness long term. Why? Well, because life gets in the way or shit happens! This is just "Earth Living." But now with the awareness that your Earth mission is to be happy and to inspire others to do the same, what do you do? You do your best!!! And know that everything is good and always working out. Go sprinkle happiness wherever you go.

Chapter 17
It Is Your Birthright to Live Joyously and Free

You came to Earth to experience Earth living, to thrive, to live every experience to the fullest; that means all experiences, including the difficult ones. You knew of the growth involved for yourself and for others. You knew that there are no tragedies, only love. You knew that our loved ones who pass on only transition into the nonphysical world but still exist. You knew you were love and that it was your birthright to live joyously and free. You knew all of the above and more.

So, let's get back to your knowing, your joy, your freedom! You ask, "How?" Smell the roses, my friend. Sip the warm tea, watch the children laughing and being free—that's what you will be when you choose to be. It comes down to choice. How do you want to live your Earth life? In prison, stuck in life situations, or free, living without constraints? Constraints are doing what others—society, parents, teachers, and the government—tell you to do rather than what your inner guidance whispers and guides you to do.

It is your birthright—you coming to Planet Earth—to live joyously and free. It is also your right to

Master Earth Living

ignore what is not true for you, what brings you down, what keeps you stuck in prison. It's your right to move away from those who are not empowering to your soul. It's your right to care about your wellbeing before others' wellbeing. That may sound insensitive, but you will notice when you take care of yourself first, others learn how to take care of themselves first as well. This is when our light grows with others' lights and our world glows with love.

It's your birthright, my friend, to be joyful, to laugh, to dance, and to flow. When you do this, you are following your own inner guidance, which is always loving and kind. This is when you find the love of your life, that amazing job lands right in your lap, you smile from ear to ear for no specific reason.

It's your birthright to know who you are, be who you are, and live as the joyous being you are. So, make that choice to live in the flow of divine love, which is you! You are an amazing light being, and it's your birthright to shine.

Chapter 18
The Art of Playing

When I was in my physical form, I loved to play, laugh, and have fun. I didn't realize until I passed why that was so important for my evolution. I just knew that it felt good. Have you ever watched a baby play in his or her own world as if no one else mattered? Unfortunately, most humans lose that playfulness by their teenage years because then they are usually well ingrained in the mainstream way of thinking, which is to work hard and then play.

How messed up is that? It should be to play hard and then work. Work would be so much more enjoyable then. Don't you agree?

What I learned about play once I returned home to Heaven was that play, joy, and laughter were necessary for our evolution because through happiness, joy, and play, you experience all the experiences you chose on a lighter note, a playful manner, not with an "Oh my God, why did this happen?" mindset. An example: you chose to experience heartache in this lifetime to learn the lesson of compassion. You actually learn from experiencing the opposite. When coming from a playful, joyful attitude, you are more strongly connected to your divine source, who is guiding you

Master Earth Living

through this experience. You are enlightened to the fact that this is one of your life lessons, and you learn and move on.

On the other hand, when you come from a place of anger and hurt when dealing with heartache, you limit yourself, as you are missing all your divine messages that enlighten and guide. You feel basically like you are on your own, operating from only the Earth mind, which is often fear based. So, when we see the bigger picture, or see situations from a Heavenly perspective, everything is so much easier to move through.

So, play and maintain that open connection with your divine guidance, as you will gracefully be assisted through all of your Earth life situations when you allow yourself to receive. In your playful, joyful mode, you are allowing and open to receive. I know I've said this before, but Earth life was never meant to be something you journey on your own! Play, open up, allow, listen, receive, and you'll love your life!

Jeremy laughing and having fun with his sisters

Chapter 19
Just Be You!

You live in a world where there are so many expectations to do this, do that, be this, and be that. It can be a bit confusing and difficult to remember who you are when you are wearing so many different hats.

Sometimes it may seem a little funny when you step back and view yourself—waiting tables, sitting in a high school health class, or cleaning up after your little brother—but ask yourself, "Is this who I really am? Am I really this? Who am I? What do I want me to be?"

Of course, we will be involved in the mundane experiences in life, but make sure you do not lose who you really are while waiting on tables or taking care of your little brother.

So, who are you? We touched on this in the first chapter; you are a spark of a higher source or God/Source energy. You can create and move mountains. You are love and compassion. You are on Earth to live your life as you and to be you, your authentic you, in all that you do.

In your life, where are you falling short with being you? In your job, in school, or within your family? What would it be like to be the true authentic you in your job, in school, and within your family? Most people seem to like honesty, even if one's honesty is difficult to agree with. How often have you heard: "At least they were being honest"?

What if you share a new menu item or another way to accomplish a task at the restaurant you work at? Great employers will respect the suggestions since trends are always changing and new ideas are helpful. If your suggestions are not well received, that might be a sign to walk out the door; to find an employer who respects new ideas and loves to keep up with what's always evolving.

My point is—live as YOU, expressing you, loving who you are, and your life will be adventurous. You will attract others who respect who they are and who you are authentic as well. They will love your talents and gifts as you will love theirs.

In a world filled with individual beings living true to themselves, you will find so much pleasure, joy, and ease. It takes lots more energy to be someone you are not than to be who you truly are! And who is in for feeling joy and ease? That's a no-brainer, right? I love you. The true you!

Chapter 20
Everything's the Way It Is Supposed to Be!

As I've said before, if you look at Earth events from Heaven, you would see that everything is as it should be! Learning, and growing, and expanding is what it's all about. You, me, we are all learning and growing from all events.

You look at the light of a candle flickering, and it's mesmerizing. It's akin to going within to the depths of your soul. It knows. Your soul knows the lessons you chose to learn in this lifetime, the roles others agreed to play in your learning, and that all is well.

It is like you are the star of your own movie. Everything revolves around you. This is the same for all others as well. We are as one as we assist one another and we are separate as we play our parts. I know this might be a bit confusing, but there's really no need to fully understand this, as your soul understands it very well and will lead you to the adventures that will arouse the awakening of the mind. Follow your intuition, as I have previously shared, as this is the soul leading you on your path. Everyone's paths are different, but our paths certainly cross and coincide. All is well and as it should be.

When you are feeling off or out of balance, ask yourself, "What am I to learn from this?" Listen, observe, take action, and grow. This will move you gently back onto your path. Feeling off is not a bad thing. It is necessary for your evolution. We learn so much about ourselves when we feel off, and no worries, this feeling is only temporary, and you will regain your purpose or why you are here soon.

So, why are you here? We've touched on this a bit already, but you are here to share your special unique gifts with the world. You are never permanently off your path. And you can shorten the "off" feeling by doing what I suggest, which is to ask, "What am I to learn?" You can also ask, "What will help me to regain my balance and return to my divine path with flow and ease?" Then be open to receive whatever comes to you in a thought, a knowing, a whisper, or a scream.

When my mom was considering quitting her social work job after 20 years, she knew she was "off" her divine path. She knew what she needed to do, but fear of the unknown, of what would happen next, kept her hostage. She will tell you she never heard her divine guidance so loudly scream, "Quit! Quit! Quit!" And with an additional push of support from my dad, she quit her job and she has never regretted that decision or looked back. Moving forward was not easy, as my mom put up great resistance, but she is pleased as to where her life led her from the day she said "I quit." Everything is the way it should be. Everything! Go with the flow and glow. Ride the tide. It's a beautiful life.

Chapter 21
Is Your Spirit Within?

When feeling low and out of sorts, your spirit is most likely not completely within or you are not paying attention to it. My mom has learned how to determine how much of one's spirit is actually attached to their body. If you have feelings of anger or depression, your spirit is out to lunch, returning only when you decide or make a choice that you want to live, really live, not just half-ass, pardon my language, but fully in. It's a detached feeling, a disconnection, a feeling of aloneness, of being lost. We've all been there.

So, what do you do? Well, first know that your spirit came to Earth to play, have fun, and to enjoy life, so why would it want to stay completely connected in a body that chooses the opposite? Spirit doesn't. And it's not like your spirit is completely detached, as your body would not be breathing if that was the case. But a great portion of your spirit may be detached, waiting for a body to choose life or living. So, to answer: What do you do?

First, choose life. Choose living. No matter what Earth circumstances may bring, choose to live. This does not mean living in sadness and sorrow. Is that really living? This means living in peace and joy.

Master Earth Living

Second, release the heavy energy blocking your joy and from being able to feel your spirit. This was touched upon previously, but it is important to address again in context of these additional tools. The emotions of hate, sadness, anger, and shame are definite blockers. Identify these heavy blocking energies and proclaim strong intentions for these energies to leave. Then allow them to leave. Energy Healing works great for releasing blocks. Another way to release heavy energy is to shower this energy with love. Love conquers all. And just a reminder that all events, all situations, all emotions, and all traumas were necessary for your evolution, so loving everything shifts energy quickly into what you desire.

Third, call your spirit back into your body by stating your request and strong intention to do so. Our spirits wait patiently for us to choose to live because they love us so much. When ready, just imagine your beautiful spirit, a beam of white light for many, entering into the crown chakra, located at the top of the head and radiating into every cell of your body and maneuvering down every chakra, which are known as Heavenly portals, balancing, cleansing, and reprogramming your body.

Fourth, as your spirit light continues down the body, ground to Mother Earth. Allow this energy to move down your legs and attach to Mother Earth. Feel her strength and guidance. Many people feel a

Master Earth Living

burst of energy rise up from their feet to their hearts and then radiate outward from their heart chakras.

Fifth, use your intention to allow your spirit light to radiate from your heart, touching as far as you allow it to reach. Your spirit energy combined with Mother Earth's energy is powerful. You might notice others around you feeling more at ease.

Sixth, stay in this amazing energy for as long as you like. You may notice feelings of happiness as anxiety dissipates and worries are erased because divine guidance is now flowing to you and through you with your spirit intact.

This is where magic occurs—when you feel and hear this divine guidance as your spirit leads the way. As the meanings of Earth events come to light, your next step is revealed, and the magic that was waiting patiently for you surfaces to delight you. You are now at ease, walking on your divine path with your spirit/divine self aligned with your human counterpart. And that, my friend, is how it is done. You are a blessing! You are magical! You are powerful! You are an eternal light spirit living joyously within a human body. Enjoy Earth life.

Chapter 22
Hear Me and Hear Me Big!

If you want to Master Earth Living, follow this procedure...

First, know who you are—an eternal, unlimited, divine being of the Universe.

Second, breathe. Breathe in the light of divine guidance and exhale the dark of doubt, worry, and disbelief.

Third, throw your hands up and let whatever be, just be! All Earth situations are for your evolution. Just let them be. Learn the lessons from them and move on.

Fourth, see what you want to see. See the good in all things, as there is always something good in everything. Focus your attention on only good.

Fifth, feel what you want to feel. Set your intention on feeling joy in all things. It's a choice.

Sixth, be who you want to be. Envision yourself as who you desire, write it down, anchor it in, and then live It!

Master Earth Living

Seven, create what you want in your life. Write it down, see it, and allow it in.

Eight, leave the "how's" to us. Just follow your divine guidance's lead and do it, do it, do it!!!

Nine, let all resistance go. That is just an Earth/ego thing, and you want to live Heaven on Earth, right?

Ten, gratitude. Be grateful for every single life experience. It's all orchestrated just for you! Gotta love it!

And there you have it—Master Earth Living 101. If you do these 10 steps, then you are Mastering Earth Living. If you are not doing these steps, ask yourself "Do I want to live my best Earth life?" If you respond "No," then ask yourself "Why not?" If "Yes," then do the 10 Steps!

It's your birthright to live in ease with what and how you want. You came to Earth knowing this. Allow this truth to resurface. Your soul already knows this truth. Do the steps and allow your ego/Earth mind to rekindle the truth! You are amazing! Now be amazing! We love and support you always!

Chapter 23
It Is Time!

Now you have the tools, the awareness, and your divine helpers, so go forth and create your beautiful life just as you desire. Make it your desire, your burning desire, to live a divine Heaven-on-Earth life—happy, in the moment, and experiencing pleasure.

We love you and want nothing less than that for you. Call on us, and we will assist. Think of us, and we are there. Breathe in our love, and we are hugging you tight. This is your amazing life journey, and it always is and always will be what you make of it.

Our desire is for you to get all that you desired before you entered into the Earth realm. You deserve it all, and it is all here for you. Ask, and it is given. Have you heard that saying before? How often do you make requests? Not often enough probably. Ask, and it is given, and give thanks along the way. So much is happening behind the scenes just for you; if you truly knew, it would knock your socks off.

Love what you have. Love where you've been. Love all your hardships, as these have made it possible for you to evolve into who you are today. And love all that is on its way to you. When you can love each and every Earth situation, you are living

Master Earth Living

Heaven on Earth. It's like we are looking through a window at all that's in front of you and the struggles you have set on your path, which you are mostly unaware of, of course. We know that when you can love everything, even the difficulties, you will remain on the path of least resistance to obtaining the joy and wonder that we see for you.

It is time to release past hardships with love; release what you thought were limitations and all of your perceived ailments. Move into that joyfulness that is rising up from deep down inside you. It's like a flower blooming. It's time to allow your Heavenly, divine gifts to surface, your glow to shine, your being to radiate and blossom. This is why you are here—to live "Heaven on Earth." This is what you requested. This is all you, baby! This is you! So live, love, and shine as you! We love and support you always!

What to Do When Your Mind Runs the Show

You probably have experienced your mind racing and the crazy, maybe degrading, and unproductive thoughts that sometimes run rampant.

What can you do to regain control?

Breathe!!

Stop what you are doing and breathe!

Breathe in light and love, counting to four.

Hold your breath, counting to four, allowing your breath to expand deeply down to your stomach.

Exhale, counting to four, letting it all go.

Repeat this process four times.

Check to see if you are now relaxed.

If not, continue with this breathing exercise a few more rounds.

When relaxed, express how you would like your attitude, situation, or life, to be. **Get clear, real clear!**

Master Earth Living

Example...

"I want my arthritis in my fingers and hands to disappear so I can paint the sunset." Say your request out loud and also write it down. Writing is great to anchor your desires!

Visualize your fingers and hands, flexible and pain free, holding the paintbrush with ease and grace, gliding across the canvas and painting the sunset!

Feel this deeply into your soul and express gratitude for your divine assistants, who are always there for you and cheering you on!

Your thoughts are now positive and in alignment with whatever you can dream.

This process is guaranteed to save you from your racing mind of lower vibrational thoughts.

At the end of this process, you will be vibrating high in the sea of love where your dreams reside to easily access all of your desires.

Practice this process to rise above your mind's negative thoughts *and* **receive all that you desire!**

Afterword by Jeremy Logue

Thank you for reading our book and sharing your love. We feel it. We are all on this journey together—growing, sharing, loving, and being. Enjoy the ride. Create great adventures and truly love your life!

We love you!

Jeremy

P.S. Write your own book! You can do whatever you like. Remember how I included two Chapter 12s? What are you waiting for? Get started on your own amazing story!

Afterword by Rhonda Crockett Logue

I hope that our book has provided enlightenment, heartfelt love, wonderful tools, and inspiration to live "Heaven on Earth." For me personally, viewing my life situations from a Heavenly perspective has been invaluable and truly lifesaving. Losing my son, Jeremy, in his physical form was devastating to say the least, but viewing the entire event through Heavenly eyes, I was able to see the blessings and growth for all involved from this divinely planned event, including the awareness that we never did lose him. I can assure you that Jeremy is quite alive and very active, as he talked me into writing his second book. LOL! Writing truly is not my favorite thing to do, but with Jeremy's guidance and love, it was a wonderful and enlightening experience, just as our first book, *Jeremy Shares His Love From Above*, was.

My wish is for each and every one of you to truly experience living Heaven on Earth!

With love and angel blessings!

Rhonda

Afterword by Mehrnaz Dehmiri

Last year, I got to meet Jeremy's family and stay in Jeremy's old room for a few days. It was at this time that I got to learn about his wonderful life on Earth. I then started reading his first book, *Jeremy Share His Love From Above*, and fell in love with all his stories.

Immediately after, I started experiencing situations and knew it was Jeremy showing me signs. For example, one day, I went to the transportation office to change my car's license plates and was unable to remove them because the screws were rusted. Plus, I could not find the right tools. I looked up to the sky and asked for help. I got a nudge to look to the opposite side of the street and, right then, I noticed Honda showroom. Now, in normal situations, I would not do this, but here I was, being guided to go there. As I drove over, I realized there was a service center, so I drove right up, and there I met the manager, whose name was Jeremy (seriously!). He got his men to use their power tools to remove my license plates and also told me to bring my new ones so they could install them. Guess what? They gave me phenomenal—and complementary—service.

Since then, my life has evolved tremendously in a super positive way, and I love co-creating with the help of my angels, especially Jeremy, who is always

Master Earth Living

there, reminding us to have fun, love, and enjoy living our Heavenly lives on Earth. I am feeling blessed and so grateful for each one of you as well as the opportunity to be on this wonderful journey with Jeremy and Rhonda.

P.S. If you have not read Jeremy's first book, I highly recommend you do since it's definitely a great, easy, fun and yet powerful book. You will love it and learn so much about yourself as I did.

With love and gratitude always,

Mehrnaz Dehmiri

Other Books by Jeremy Logue

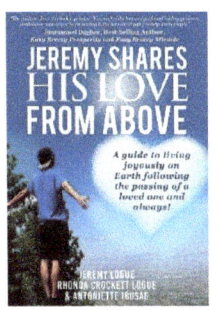

Jeremy Sends His Love From Above: A guide to living joyously on Earth following the passing of a loved one and always!

By Jeremy Logue, Rhonda Crockett Logue, and Antoniette Ibusag

An inspiring and wonderful book about living a joyous life while rising above grief from a loved one's passing. Jeremy channels his wisdom from Heaven to his mother and girlfriend. He provides the enlightenment and tools necessary to live a peaceful life on Earth--a life that we all deserve!

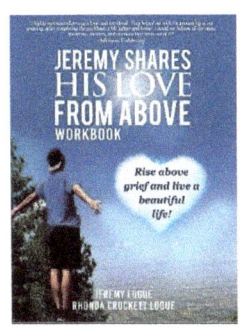

Jeremy Sends His Love From Above Workbook

By Jeremy Logue and Rhonda Crockett Logue

This workbook allows readers to reflect on thoughts and feelings about grief. With this workbook, readers are able to internalize the story of Jeremy to guide thoughtful expression with the writing prompts provided.

www.ingramcontent.com/pod-product-compliance
Lightning Source LLC
Chambersburg PA
CBHW042118100526
44587CB00025B/4109